MAKE A WIND VANE

Written by Jillian Powell

This is a wind vane.

A wind vane spins to tell us if the wind comes from:

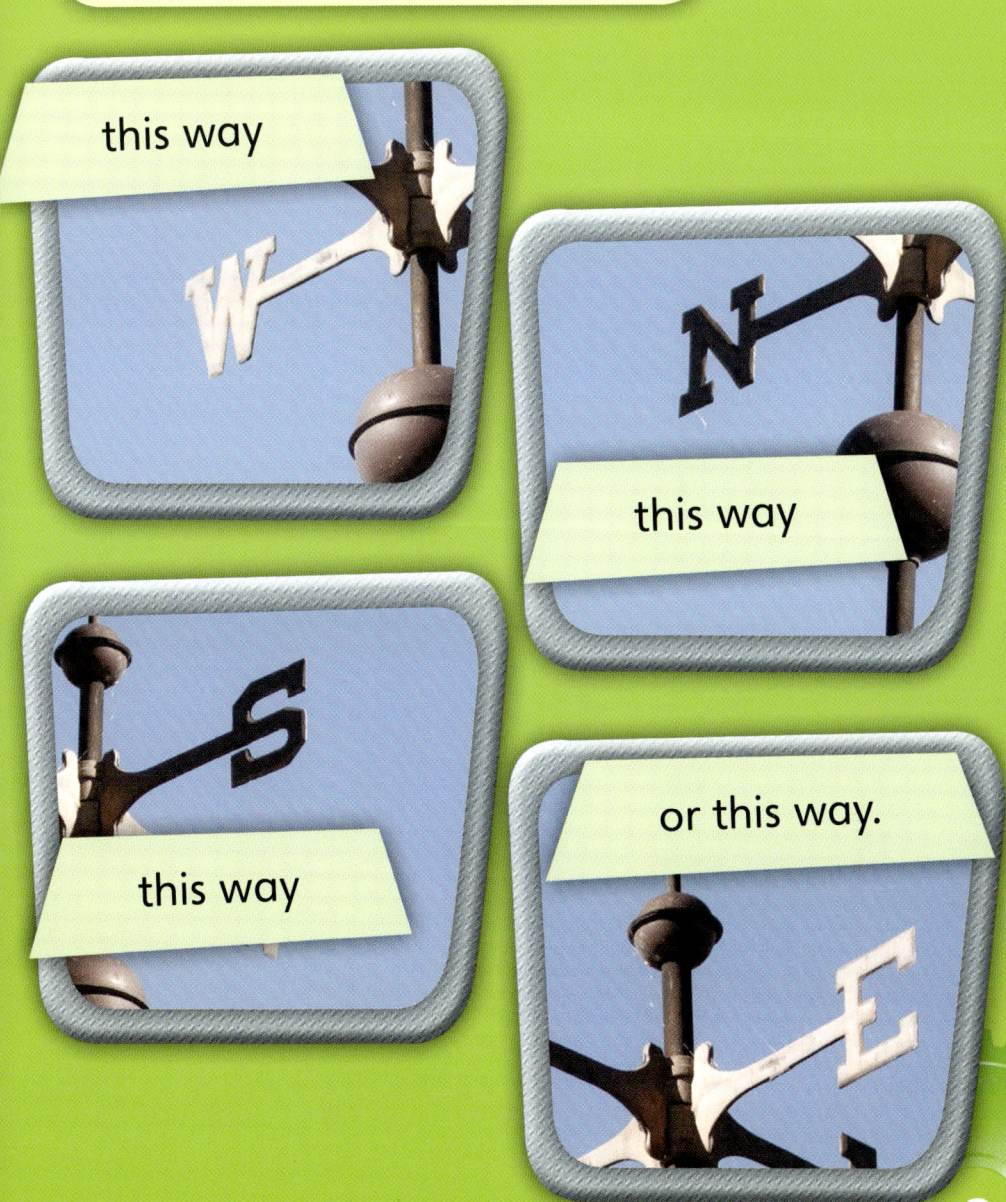

this way

this way

this way

or this way.

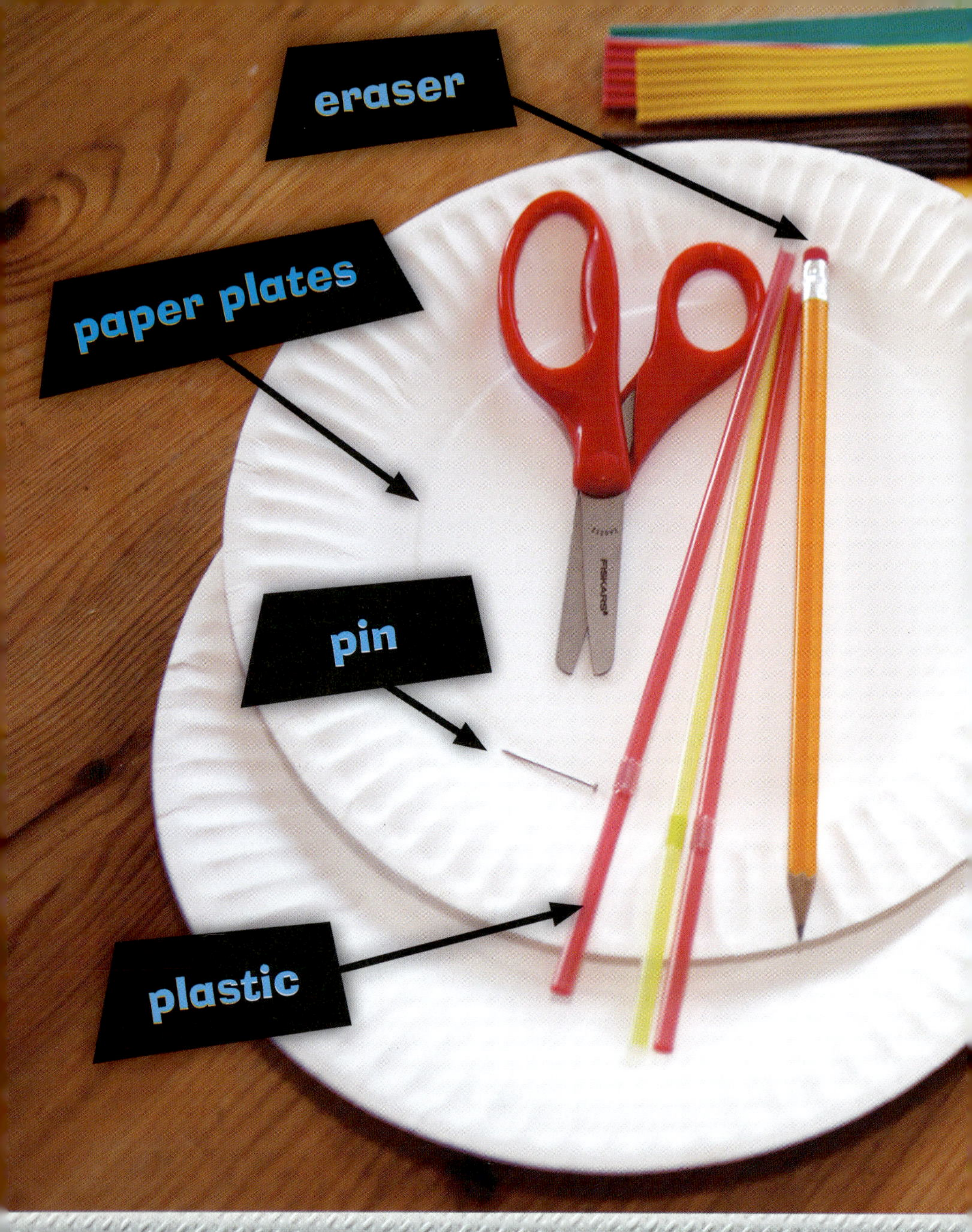

eraser

paper plates

pin

plastic

You can make a wind vane.

Collect the things you will need.

Decorate a paper plate with paints or pens.

Put the letters N, S, E and W onto the plate.

Take the display card and cut a pointed shape.

Next, make two cuts in the ends of the plastic.
They are for the card.

Push the card shape into a cut so the point is going this way.

tail shape

Next, cut a tail shape.

Push it into the cut at the end so it points this way.

Push the pin through here.

Next, push the pin into the eraser.

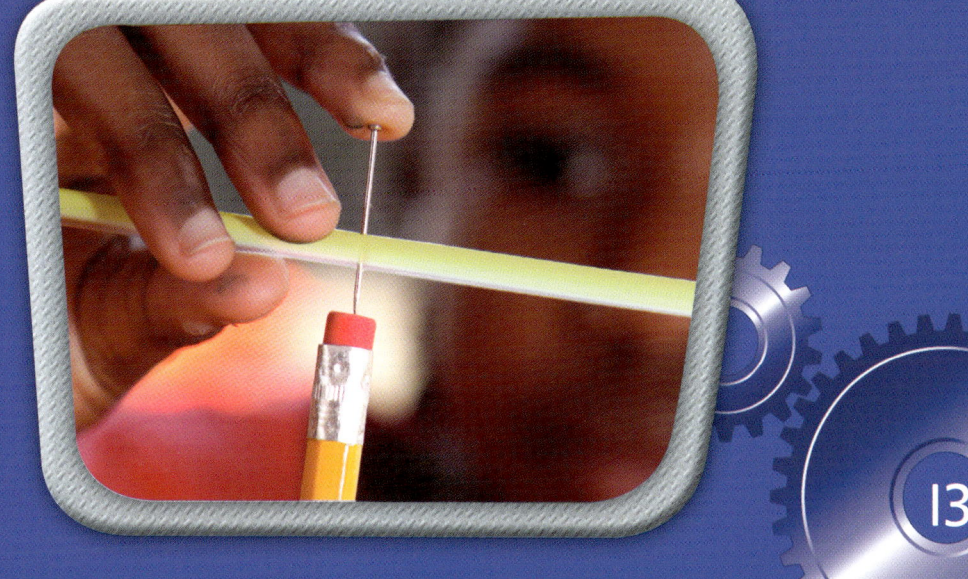

Put the clay onto the plain plate to make a base.

Push the point through the painted plate into the clay.
Pull off some tape.
Tape the top plate down.

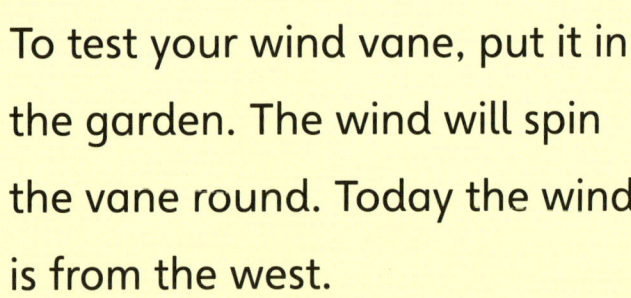

To test your wind vane, put it in the garden. The wind will spin the vane round. Today the wind is from the west.